Daniel Kahneman

Decoding the Mind, Unveiling the Secrets of Decision-Making

By

Neil Potter

About the author

Neil Potter, the author of "Daniel Kahneman: Decoding the Mind, Unveiling the Secrets of Decision-Making," is an accomplished writer and researcher dedicated to unraveling the complexities of human cognition. With a keen interest in the intersection of psychology and economics, Potter brings a passion for communicating profound ideas to a broad audience.

As an avid scholar of decision science, Potter has delved into the life and work of Daniel Kahneman, a Nobel laureate and pioneering figure in the field. Through meticulous research and an engaging narrative style, Potter seeks to convey the depth of Kahneman's contributions, making behavioral science accessible to readers of all backgrounds.

Beyond his work as an author, Neil Potter is known for his commitment to promoting a deeper understanding of the human mind. His writing reflects a dedication to bridging the gap between academic research and public awareness, aiming to inspire curiosity and spark conversations about the intricacies of decision-making.

"Daniel Kahneman: Decoding the Mind, Unveiling the Secrets of Decision-Making" is not just a book; it's a journey into the fascinating realm of behavioral economics guided by Neil Potter's passion for unraveling the mysteries of the mind.

Daniel Kahneman

Appreciation

Dear Reader,

Thank you for embarking on this intellectual journey with "Daniel Kahneman: Decoding the Mind, Unveiling the Secrets of Decision-Making." Your decision to explore the complexities of human cognition and the transformative ideas of Daniel Kahneman is sincerely appreciated.

As an author, I am deeply gratified that you have chosen to delve into the pages of this book. Through meticulous research and a passion for conveying profound concepts, my aim is to make the world of behavioral economics accessible and intriguing. Daniel Kahneman's groundbreaking work has reshaped our understanding of decision-making, and your commitment to exploring these insights adds a valuable dimension to the ongoing conversation.

I invite you to immerse yourself in the narrative, discovering the life, contributions, and enduring legacy of Daniel Kahneman. May this exploration stimulate your curiosity, spark thoughtful contemplation, and provide you with a deeper appreciation for the intricacies of the human mind.

Once again, thank you for choosing "Daniel Kahneman." Your support is a testament to the enduring relevance of exploring the intersection of psychology and economics, and I am delighted to have you as a fellow traveler on this intellectual voyage.

With gratitude,

Neil Potter

Copyright

Dedication

To the Pioneers of Thought,
whose insatiable curiosity
illuminates the corridors of understanding.

To the Seekers of Knowledge,
whose journey transcends pages
and embraces the profound.

To Daniel Kahneman,
whose intellectual legacy
continues to shape the landscape of our
minds.

This book is dedicated to those
who question, ponder, and explore,
for in the pursuit of wisdom,
we find the true essence of being.

— Neil Potter

Daniel Kahneman

Table of contents

Daniel Kahneman

Daniel Kahneman

Chapter Nine: Personal Life

Family and personal experiences

Balancing work and life

Chapter Ten: Conclusion

Summary of key points

Final thoughts on Daniel Kahneman's life and contributions

Awards and recognition

Introduction

In the realm of psychology and economics, few figures have left an indelible mark as profound as Daniel Kahneman. Born into a world of intellectual curiosity and shaped by the crucible of life experiences, Kahneman's journey unfolds as a testament to the power of a singular mind in transforming our understanding of decision-making and human behavior.

As we embark on this biographical exploration, we peel back the layers of Kahneman's early life, tracing the roots of his inquisitive nature and the formative moments that laid the foundation for a groundbreaking career. From the labyrinth of academia to the crucible of collaborative research, Kahneman's trajectory takes us through the corridors of groundbreaking discoveries and paradigm-shifting insights.

The narrative weaves through the tapestry of Kahneman's accomplishments, punctuated by the pinnacle moment – the Nobel Prize in Economics. A laureate who transcended disciplines, his work in prospect theory reshaped the landscape of behavioral economics, leaving an enduring imprint on how we perceive decision-making in both individual and collective contexts.

Yet, beyond the laurels and accolades lies the heart of this narrative – "Thinking, Fast and Slow." The seminal work that beckons readers to traverse the corridors of the mind, exploring the dual systems that govern our thoughts and choices. This book, a cornerstone in Kahneman's legacy, serves as a portal into the intricate workings of the human psyche, inviting us to grapple with the complexities that define our cognitive landscape.

However, the brilliance of Kahneman does not rest solely in his individual genius. The narrative delves into the collaborative dance with Amos Tversky, a partnership that birthed insights transcending the sum of its parts. Together, they navigated the uncharted waters of behavioral science, leaving an enduring legacy that extends far beyond the confines of research papers and scholarly accolades.

As we journey through Kahneman's later career, we witness the evolution of his ideas and their impact on real-world decision-making. The pages unfold to reveal a man who not only dissected the intricacies of the human mind but also sought to bridge the chasm between theory and application.

Personal anecdotes and glimpses into Kahneman's family life add a human touch to the narrative, portraying a multifaceted personality whose pursuits extended beyond the hallowed halls of academia. We explore the delicate balance between the personal and professional, providing a holistic perspective on the man behind the theories.

In the twilight of this biography, reflections from Kahneman himself offer insights into a life lived in pursuit of understanding the human condition. His thoughts on his own journey, the lessons learned, and the path forward resonate as a coda to a symphony of intellectual brilliance.

This biography endeavors to encapsulate not only the chronological unfolding of a remarkable life but also the essence of Daniel Kahneman's impact on the fields of psychology and economics. As we turn the pages, we invite readers to embark on a journey through the corridors of thought, guided by a luminary whose work continues to shape our understanding of the human experience.

Background on Daniel Kahneman

Daniel Kahneman, born on March 5, 1934, in Tel Aviv, Israel, emerged from a childhood marked by the tumultuous backdrop of World War II. Raised in the crucible of uncertainty, his formative years were shaped by the pervasive challenges of wartime existence. This early exposure to unpredictability and decision-making in the face of adversity would later become a cornerstone of his research.

Kahneman's intellectual journey began at the Hebrew University of Jerusalem, where he delved into the study of psychology. It was during these academic pursuits that he first grappled with the intricacies of the human mind, laying the groundwork for a career that would redefine the intersection of psychology and economics.

His early interests in the workings of the mind led him to pursue a Ph.D. in Psychology at the University of California,

Berkeley. This academic sojourn in the United States exposed Kahneman to a diverse intellectual landscape, fostering the cross-pollination of ideas that would later characterize his groundbreaking work.

Returning to Israel, Kahneman embarked on a career in academia, initially focusing on issues related to visual perception. However, it was a fortuitous shift to the study of decision-making and behavioral economics that catapulted him into the spotlight. Collaborating with Amos Tversky, their partnership would prove transformative, laying the groundwork for seminal contributions that continue to reverberate across disciplines.

As we unravel the layers of Kahneman's early life, we discover a thinker whose roots in a world marked by upheaval and intellectual curiosity set the stage for a career that would reshape the very foundations of how we understand human behavior and decision-making.

Significance of his contributions to psychology and economics

Daniel Kahneman's contributions to psychology and economics are monumental, shaping the way we perceive decision-making and human behavior. His work has had a profound impact on both fields, and the significance of his contributions can be summarized as follows:

- **Prospect Theory and Behavioral Economics:**

Kahneman's groundbreaking development of prospect theory challenged traditional economic models, introducing the concept of behavioral economics.

Prospect theory demonstrated that individuals' decisions are influenced by perceived gains and losses, rather than following strict rationality as assumed by classical economic theories.

- **Dual System of Thinking:**

The distinction between System 1 (fast, intuitive) and System 2 (slow, deliberate) thinking, as outlined in "Thinking, Fast and Slow," revolutionized cognitive psychology.

This dual-system framework provides a comprehensive understanding of how people make decisions, incorporating both automatic and reflective processes.

- **Nobel Prize in Economics:**

Awarded the Nobel Prize in Economic Sciences in 2002, Kahneman became the first psychologist to receive this honor, recognizing the profound impact of his work on economic theory and decision-making.

- **Collaboration with Amos Tversky:**

Kahneman's collaboration with Amos Tversky produced influential research that challenged conventional assumptions about rational decision-making.

Their work highlighted cognitive biases, heuristics, and systematic errors that influence human judgment, paving the way for a more realistic and nuanced understanding of economic behavior.

• **Real-world Applications:**

Kahneman's research has transcended academia, influencing diverse fields such as finance, public policy, and organizational management.

Practical applications of his insights have led to improvements in decision-making processes, risk management, and the design of public policies.

• **Popularization of Behavioral Science:**

Through "Thinking, Fast and Slow," Kahneman brought complex psychological concepts to a broader audience, popularizing behavioral science and making it accessible to the general public.

This accessibility has fostered a wider understanding of how cognitive biases impact daily decision-making.

- **Impact on Policy and Regulation:**

Kahneman's work has informed policy discussions and regulatory frameworks, particularly in areas such as finance, healthcare, and environmental decision-making.

Policymakers now consider the psychological aspects of decision-making when designing interventions and regulations.

In essence, Daniel Kahneman's contributions have not only reshaped academic disciplines but have also permeated into practical realms, influencing how individuals, organizations, and societies approach decision-making. His work continues to be a guiding force in understanding the complexities of the human mind and improving the quality of decision processes on both individual and societal levels.

Chapter One: Early Life

Daniel Kahneman's early life unfolded against the backdrop of historic events, significantly shaping the trajectory of his intellectual journey:

- **World War II and Childhood in Israel:**

Born on March 5, 1934, in Tel Aviv, Israel, Kahneman's early years were marked by the tumultuous atmosphere of World War II.

The challenges of wartime existence provided a unique backdrop, exposing him to the complexities of decision-making in uncertain and adverse conditions.

- **Intellectual Curiosity and Educational Background:**

Kahneman's intellectual curiosity emerged early in life, prompting him to explore the workings of the mind from a young age.

He pursued his higher education at the Hebrew University of Jerusalem, where he began delving into the field of psychology, setting the stage for his future contributions.

- **Move to the United States and Doctoral Studies:**

In pursuit of furthering his academic pursuits, Kahneman ventured to the United States for doctoral studies in Psychology at the University of California, Berkeley.

This period exposed him to a diverse intellectual environment, fostering the cross-pollination of ideas that would later characterize his interdisciplinary approach.

- **Academic Exploration and Early Research:**

Kahneman's early academic career initially focused on issues related to visual perception, reflecting a broad interest in the intricacies of human cognition.

It was during these early years that he began to explore the foundations of decision-making, setting the stage for his transformative shift into the realm of behavioral economics.

- **Return to Israel and Academic Career:**

Following his time in the United States, Kahneman returned to Israel and embarked on an academic career.

His initial contributions laid the groundwork for later groundbreaking research, and his collaboration with Amos Tversky, a fellow psychologist, would prove pivotal in shaping the landscape of behavioral economics.

In essence, Daniel Kahneman's early life reveals the interplay of personal experiences, intellectual curiosity, and the evolving geopolitical landscape. These formative years laid the groundwork for a career that would revolutionize our understanding of decision-making and human behavior, making him a towering figure in the fields of psychology and economics.

Childhood and upbringing

Daniel Kahneman's childhood and upbringing played a crucial role in shaping the foundation of his intellectual curiosity and resilience:

- **Early Years in Tel Aviv:**

Born on March 5, 1934, in Tel Aviv, Israel, Kahneman spent his formative years in a city shaped by the cultural and geopolitical dynamics of the time.

The backdrop of World War II and its impact on daily life likely instilled a sense of adaptability and resilience.

- **Influence of Wartime Adversity:**

The wartime adversity in Tel Aviv provided Kahneman with firsthand exposure to uncertainty and decision-making in challenging circumstances.

These early experiences likely influenced his later interest in understanding how individuals navigate and make choices in complex and unpredictable situations.

- **Intellectual Curiosity and Early Learning:**

Kahneman's intellectual curiosity emerged early, prompting him to explore the workings of the mind and human behavior.

His early experiences and learning environment may have fostered a keen interest in understanding the psychological underpinnings of decision-making.

- **Educational Path:**

As he progressed through his education, Kahneman's intellectual pursuits led him to the Hebrew University of Jerusalem, where he began to delve into the field of psychology.

The early seeds of his interest in understanding human cognition were likely sown during this period.

- **Impact of Family and Surroundings:**

The influence of family dynamics and the cultural milieu of Tel Aviv during his upbringing likely contributed to Kahneman's holistic understanding of human behavior.

The support and encouragement from family members may have played a role in nurturing his academic pursuits.

- **Resilience and Adaptability:**

The challenging times of Kahneman's childhood, including the wartime context, may have instilled in him a sense of resilience and adaptability.

These qualities could have been instrumental in his ability to navigate complex intellectual terrain and pursue groundbreaking research later in life.

In essence, Daniel Kahneman's childhood and upbringing laid the groundwork for a career marked by intellectual curiosity, a deep understanding of decision-making under uncertainty, and a resilience that would shape his contributions to psychology and economics. The interplay of personal experiences and environmental influences during his early years provided a unique backdrop for the emergence of a visionary thinker.

Educational background and early interests

Daniel Kahneman's educational background and early interests provide insights into the formative years that shaped his intellectual journey:

- **Hebrew University of Jerusalem:**

Kahneman pursued his higher education at the Hebrew University of Jerusalem, where he began his academic journey in the field of psychology.

This early exposure to the study of the mind laid the foundation for his lifelong fascination with human behavior and decision-making.

- **Doctoral Studies at UC Berkeley:**

In pursuit of furthering his understanding of psychology, Kahneman moved to the United States for doctoral studies at the University of California, Berkeley.

This period marked a crucial juncture in his education, exposing him to a diverse academic environment and fostering interdisciplinary perspectives.

- **Shift from Visual Perception to Decision-Making:**

Initially focusing on visual perception in his academic pursuits, Kahneman's interests evolved over time.

The transition from studying visual perception to delving into the complexities of decision-making marked a pivotal shift that would define the trajectory of his groundbreaking contributions.

- **Intellectual Curiosity and Broad Interests:**

Kahneman's early interests reflected a broad curiosity about the workings of the human mind.

His intellectual pursuits went beyond the confines of a single discipline, paving the way for interdisciplinary approaches that would later characterize his collaboration with Amos Tversky.

- **Exploration of Cognitive Biases:**

As his academic career progressed, Kahneman began exploring cognitive biases and systematic errors in human decision-making.

This exploration laid the groundwork for the development of prospect theory, a seminal contribution that challenged traditional economic models.

- **Collaboration with Amos Tversky:**

One of the most influential chapters in Kahneman's early career was his collaboration with Amos Tversky.

Together, they conducted groundbreaking research that dissected the nuances of human judgment and decision-making, contributing significantly to the field of behavioral economics.

In summary, Daniel Kahneman's educational journey reflects a trajectory from foundational studies in psychology to a pioneering exploration of decision-making processes. His early interests, interdisciplinary approach, and collaboration with like-minded thinkers set the stage for a career that would reshape our understanding of human cognition and behavior.

Daniel Kahneman's career beginnings mark the commencement of a journey that would redefine the fields of psychology and economics:

- **Academic Path in Israel:**

After completing his doctoral studies at the University of California, Berkeley, Kahneman returned to Israel to embark on an academic career.

His early contributions in academia laid the groundwork for the exploration of decision-making and behavioral economics.

- **Initial Focus on Visual Perception:**

Kahneman's early academic pursuits initially centered on visual perception, showcasing a broad interest in the complexities of human cognition.

This early focus set the stage for the later integration of psychological insights into economic decision-making.

- **Transition to Decision-Making Research:**

A pivotal moment in Kahneman's career was the transition from studying visual perception to delving into decision-making processes.

This shift marked the beginning of his exploration into the psychological underpinnings of choices and judgments.

- **Collaboration with Amos Tversky:**

One of the most significant developments in Kahneman's early career was his collaboration with Amos Tversky, a partnership that would prove transformative.

Together, they conducted groundbreaking research that challenged conventional economic theories and laid the foundation for behavioral economics.

• **Formation of Prospect Theory:**

Kahneman's collaboration with Tversky led to the development of prospect theory, a seminal contribution that revolutionized the understanding of how individuals evaluate and choose between different outcomes.

Prospect theory introduced the concept of loss aversion and highlighted the impact of cognitive biases on decision-making.

• **Recognition in Academic Circles:**

As their research gained recognition, Kahneman and Tversky's work began to influence academic circles, challenging established norms in psychology and economics.

Their innovative approach to studying human judgment and decision-making set the stage for a paradigm shift in these fields.

- **Influence on Behavioral Economics:**

Kahneman's early career laid the groundwork for the emergence of behavioral economics as a distinct and influential field.

His research challenged the rational choice model, demonstrating the role of psychological factors in economic decision-making.

In summary, the early phase of Daniel Kahneman's career was marked by a transition from visual perception research to a pioneering exploration of decision-making processes. The collaboration with Amos Tversky and the formulation of prospect theory were instrumental in shaping the trajectory of his influential and transformative contributions to psychology and economics.

Entry into psychology and academia

Daniel Kahneman's entry into psychology and academia marked the beginning of a journey that would redefine our understanding of decision-making and human behavior:

- **Educational Foundation:**

Kahneman's journey into psychology started with his educational foundation at the Hebrew University of Jerusalem.

His early academic pursuits laid the groundwork for his interest in the complexities of the human mind.

- **Doctoral Studies in the United States:**

Motivated by a thirst for deeper knowledge, Kahneman pursued doctoral studies in psychology at the University of California, Berkeley.

This move to the United States exposed him to a diverse academic environment, contributing to the interdisciplinary perspectives that would shape his later work.

- **Broad Academic Interests:**

During his early academic years, Kahneman demonstrated a broad range of interests that extended beyond traditional disciplinary boundaries.

This interdisciplinary approach would become a hallmark of his later collaboration with Amos Tversky.

- **Return to Israel:**

After completing his studies in the U.S., Kahneman returned to Israel, where he embarked on an academic career.

His early years in academia were marked by a focus on visual perception, reflecting his initial research interests.

- **Transition to Decision-Making Research:**

A pivotal moment in Kahneman's entry into psychology was the gradual shift from visual perception research to the exploration of decision-making processes.

This transition marked the beginning of his groundbreaking work on the psychological aspects of decision-making.

- **Influence of Cognitive Psychology:**

Kahneman's academic trajectory was influenced by the emerging field of cognitive psychology, which provided a framework for understanding mental processes such as perception, memory, and decision-making.

His work would later bridge the gap between cognitive psychology and economic decision theory.

- **Collaboration with Amos Tversky:**

The turning point in Kahneman's entry into psychology was his collaboration with Amos Tversky.

Together, they formed a dynamic partnership that would produce groundbreaking research, challenging conventional economic models and reshaping the landscape of decision science.

In summary, Daniel Kahneman's entry into psychology and academia was characterized by a journey from foundational education to the exploration of decision-making processes. His interdisciplinary approach and collaboration with Tversky laid the groundwork for a career that would leave an indelible mark on the fields of psychology and economics.

Collaborations and notable early research

Daniel Kahneman's early career was marked by collaborations and notable research that laid the groundwork for his groundbreaking contributions to psychology and economics:

- **Collaboration with Amos Tversky:**

The collaboration between Kahneman and Tversky began in the late 1960s and proved to be one of the most influential partnerships in the history of behavioral science.

Their synergy and complementary skills resulted in a series of groundbreaking studies that challenged traditional economic models and introduced new insights into decision-making.

• **Cognitive Biases and Heuristics:**

Kahneman and Tversky's early research focused on revealing systematic biases in human judgment and decision-making.

The identification of cognitive biases, such as anchoring and availability heuristics, highlighted the departure from the rational decision-making assumptions prevalent in classical economics.

• **Prospect Theory:**

One of the duo's seminal achievements was the development of prospect theory, introduced in 1979.

Prospect theory revolutionized our understanding of how individuals make decisions under uncertainty, emphasizing the role of perceived gains and losses rather than objective outcomes.

- ## **The Conjunction Fallacy:**

Kahneman and Tversky explored the conjunction fallacy, where people incorrectly judge the probability of two events occurring together to be higher than the probability of either event occurring alone.

This research demonstrated the systematic errors in human reasoning and decision-making.

- ## **Endowment Effect:**

The duo also contributed to the understanding of the endowment effect, where individuals tend to assign higher value to items merely because they own them.

This phenomenon challenged traditional economic theories of value.

- **Influence on Behavioral Economics:**

Kahneman and Tversky's collaborative research laid the foundation for the emergence of behavioral economics as a field.

Their work provided a psychological perspective on economic decision-making, prompting a shift from the traditional rational choice model.

- **Recognition and Impact:**

The collaborative research of Kahneman and Tversky gained widespread recognition within academic circles.

Their findings influenced various disciplines, from economics to psychology, sparking a paradigm shift in how researchers and practitioners approached the study of human behavior.

In summary, Kahneman's collaborations, particularly with Amos Tversky, produced a body of early research that revealed fundamental insights into human decision-making. This collaborative effort set the stage for Kahneman's later individual contributions and the transformative impact on the fields of psychology and economics.

Chapter Three: Groundbreaking Work: Prospect Theory

Daniel Kahneman and Amos Tversky's groundbreaking work on Prospect Theory, introduced in 1979, stands as a cornerstone in behavioral economics and psychology. Here are key aspects of this seminal contribution:

- **Conceptual Revolution:**

Prospect Theory represented a conceptual revolution in understanding how individuals make decisions under conditions of uncertainty.

It departed from traditional economic theories, challenging the assumption of rational decision-making and introducing a more psychologically nuanced model.

- **Gains and Losses:**

The theory focused on how individuals perceive and evaluate potential outcomes in terms of gains and losses relative to a reference point.

It introduced the concept of diminishing sensitivity, illustrating that people are more sensitive to changes in probability and value for small outcomes than large ones.

- **Value Function:**

The Value Function, a key element of Prospect Theory, depicted how individuals subjectively weigh gains and losses.

Loss aversion, where losses loom larger than equivalent gains, was a central insight, challenging traditional economic assumptions of symmetry in decision-making.

- **Reflection of Real-World Behavior:**

Prospect Theory was developed based on empirical observations of how people actually make decisions in various contexts.

Its empirical foundation and descriptive accuracy distinguished it from normative economic models, reflecting the complexities of human decision-making in the real world.

- **Impact on Behavioral Economics:**

The theory played a pivotal role in the formation of behavioral economics, a field that integrates psychological insights into economic analysis.

Prospect Theory demonstrated that individuals deviate from strict rationality, incorporating psychological factors that influence decision processes.

- **Application to Risk and Uncertainty:**

Kahneman and Tversky's work demonstrated that individuals exhibit risk aversion in the domain of gains but risk-seeking behavior in the domain of losses.

This finding had profound implications for understanding financial decision-making, investment behavior, and risk management.

- **Recognition and Nobel Prize:**

The impact of Prospect Theory was widely recognized, earning Kahneman the Nobel Prize in Economic Sciences in 2002.

The Nobel Committee acknowledged how the theory had transformed the way economists and psychologists think about decision-making.

- **Continued Influence:**

Prospect Theory remains highly influential, shaping research in diverse fields and influencing decision-making models in finance, public policy, and beyond.

Its enduring impact underscores the significance of Kahneman and Tversky's groundbreaking work.

In summary, Prospect Theory revolutionized our understanding of decision-making by providing a nuanced and empirically grounded model that considers the psychological dimensions of gains, losses, and risk. This theory not only marked a paradigm shift but also laid the foundation for subsequent developments in the interdisciplinary field of behavioral economics.

Development of prospect theory

The development of Prospect Theory by Daniel Kahneman and Amos Tversky represents a landmark in the understanding of decision-making under uncertainty. Here is a chronological overview of the key stages in the development of Prospect Theory:

- **Early Collaborations:**

Kahneman and Tversky's collaboration began in the late 1960s, where they explored cognitive biases and heuristics influencing decision-making.

Their joint efforts laid the groundwork for a series of studies that would ultimately lead to the formulation of Prospect Theory.

- **Decision Under Uncertainty (1974):**

In a seminal paper titled "Judgment under Uncertainty: Heuristics and Biases" (1974), Kahneman and Tversky examined how individuals make decisions when faced with uncertain information.

This paper introduced concepts like representativeness heuristic and availability heuristic, providing insights into systematic errors in judgment.

- **Prospect Theory Framework (1979):**

The culmination of their collaborative efforts resulted in the publication of "Prospect Theory: An Analysis of Decision under Risk" in 1979.

This groundbreaking paper presented the framework of Prospect Theory, challenging traditional economic models by incorporating psychological elements into decision-making.

- **Key Components of Prospect Theory:**

Value Function: Introduced the S-shaped value function that describes how individuals evaluate gains and losses relative to a reference point.

Diminishing Sensitivity: Highlighted that people are less sensitive to changes in probability and value for large outcomes compared to small ones.

Loss Aversion: Established that losses loom larger than equivalent gains, illustrating a fundamental asymmetry in decision-making.

- **Empirical Basis:**

Prospect Theory was developed based on empirical observations and experiments conducted by Kahneman and Tversky.

Their research involved eliciting people's preferences in various decision scenarios, providing a robust empirical foundation for the proposed theory.

- **Departure from Expected Utility Theory:**

Prospect Theory represented a departure from the normative assumptions of expected utility theory, which had been the prevailing economic model.

The theory acknowledged that individuals' decisions are influenced by cognitive biases and emotional responses, challenging the assumption of purely rational decision-makers.

- **Impact and Recognition:**

The publication of Prospect Theory had a profound impact on both psychology and economics.

The framework provided a more accurate depiction of how people make decisions, and its influence extended to various disciplines, eventually earning Kahneman the Nobel Prize in Economic Sciences in 2002.

- **Legacy and Continued Influence:**

Prospect Theory's enduring legacy is reflected in its continued influence on decision research, behavioral economics, and practical applications in fields such as finance, policy, and marketing.

Its principles continue to shape our understanding of human decision-making in diverse contexts.

In summary, the development of Prospect Theory was a collaborative and iterative process that evolved from Kahneman and Tversky's early investigations into decision under uncertainty. The resulting theory not only transformed academic disciplines but also left an indelible mark on how we perceive and study decision-making in the real world.

Impact on behavioral economics

Daniel Kahneman's work, particularly Prospect Theory, has had a profound impact on the field of behavioral economics, transforming how economists and psychologists understand and model decision-making. Here are key aspects of its impact:

- **Challenging Rational Choice Models:**

Kahneman's work challenged the traditional economic assumption of rational decision-makers.

Behavioral economics emerged as a response to incorporate psychological insights into economic models, acknowledging that individuals often deviate from purely rational behavior.

- **Incorporating Psychological Factors:**

Prospect Theory incorporated psychological factors, such as loss aversion and reference dependence, into economic decision-making models.

This integration provided a more realistic representation of how individuals assess risks, make choices, and respond to gains and losses.

- **Empirical Validity:**

The empirical foundation of Kahneman's work, based on extensive experimentation, provided behavioral economics with a solid empirical grounding.

Experimental evidence supporting Prospect Theory's predictions demonstrated its applicability to real-world decision scenarios.

• **Asymmetry in Decision-Making:**

The recognition of loss aversion, where losses have a more significant impact than equivalent gains, highlighted an asymmetry in decision-making.

Behavioral economics embraced this asymmetry as a key insight, influencing discussions on risk-taking behavior and financial decision-making.

• **Heuristics and Biases:**

Kahneman and Tversky's earlier research on heuristics and biases became foundational to behavioral economics.

Concepts like anchoring, availability heuristic, and representativeness heuristic provided a framework for understanding systematic errors in judgment.

- **Behavioral Finance:**

Prospect Theory's influence extended significantly into the field of behavioral finance.

The theory explained phenomena like the disposition effect, where individuals are more likely to sell winning stocks and hold onto losing ones, challenging the efficient market hypothesis.

- **Policy Implications:**

The insights from behavioral economics have influenced public policy, as policymakers recognize the importance of understanding how individuals make decisions.

Nudges and interventions based on behavioral principles have been employed to improve outcomes in areas like healthcare, finance, and environmental conservation.

- **Integration into Economic Models:**

Behavioral economics has become an integral part of economic research and policymaking.

Researchers now routinely incorporate behavioral insights into economic models, leading to a more comprehensive understanding of decision-making processes.

- **Interdisciplinary Collaboration:**

The collaboration between psychologists like Kahneman and economists fostered interdisciplinary dialogue and collaboration.

This collaboration has enriched both fields, fostering a more holistic approach to studying human behavior and decision-making.

In summary, Daniel Kahneman's impact on behavioral economics is transformative, challenging traditional economic paradigms and enriching the field with insights from psychology. His work has influenced how economists model decision processes, understand biases, and design policies that align with the realities of human behavior.

Chapter Four: Nobel Prize in Economics

Daniel Kahneman was awarded the Sveriges Riksbank Prize in Economic Sciences in Memory of Alfred Nobel, commonly referred to as the Nobel Prize in Economics, in 2002. Here are key points about his Nobel Prize:

- **Recognition of Behavioral Economics:**

Kahneman received the Nobel Prize for his groundbreaking work in integrating insights from psychological research into economic science.

The prize acknowledged his pivotal role in developing behavioral economics and challenging traditional economic models that assumed rational decision-making.

- **First Psychologist to Win the Nobel Prize in Economics:**

Kahneman's Nobel Prize marked a historic moment as he became the first psychologist to receive the award in economic sciences.

This recognition reflected the growing influence of behavioral economics and the acknowledgment of the interdisciplinary nature of his work.

- **Contributions to Decision-Making Research:**

The Nobel Committee highlighted Kahneman's contributions to understanding how individuals make decisions, especially under uncertainty and the influence of psychological factors.

Prospect Theory, with its emphasis on loss aversion and deviations from rational choice theory, was a central aspect of his recognized work.

- **Collaboration with Amos Tversky:**

While the Nobel Prize is awarded to individuals, the committee acknowledged Kahneman's collaboration with Amos Tversky.The partnership between Kahneman and Tversky was instrumental in producing groundbreaking research that significantly influenced decision science.

- **Impact on Policy and Practice:**

The Nobel Committee recognized the real-world impact of Kahneman's work, noting its relevance to policy-making and practical applications.

Concepts like prospect theory and behavioral insights have been utilized in designing policies and interventions in areas such as finance, healthcare, and public policy.

- **Validation of Behavioral Economics:**

The Nobel Prize in Economics for Kahneman validated the legitimacy and importance of behavioral economics as a distinct and influential field within economics.

It signaled a broader acceptance of the role of psychology in shaping economic decision-making.

- **Global Recognition:**

The Nobel Prize brought global attention to Kahneman's contributions and elevated the visibility of behavioral economics on the international stage.

It underscored the significance of understanding human behavior in economic contexts.

In summary, Daniel Kahneman's Nobel Prize in Economics is a testament to his transformative impact on the field. The recognition of behavioral economics and the incorporation of psychological insights into economic models were central themes in acknowledging Kahneman's groundbreaking contributions.

Recognition and significance

Daniel Kahneman's recognition and significance in the fields of psychology and economics stem from his transformative contributions, particularly in the development of behavioral economics. Here are key aspects that highlight his recognition and impact:

- **Nobel Prize in Economic Sciences (2002):**

Kahneman's receipt of the Nobel Prize in Economic Sciences marked a historic moment, as he became the first psychologist to be honored with this prestigious award.

The prize acknowledged his groundbreaking work in integrating psychological insights into economic science, challenging traditional models and reshaping the understanding of decision-making.

- **Prospect Theory and Behavioral Economics:**

Prospect Theory, developed by Kahneman and Amos Tversky, revolutionized the field of economics by introducing a psychological perspective to decision-making under uncertainty.

This work laid the foundation for behavioral economics, a field that has since gained prominence and transformed how economists study human behavior.

- **Challenging Rational Choice Models:**

Kahneman's research challenged the prevailing assumption of rational decision-making in traditional economic models.

The acknowledgment of systematic biases, heuristics, and emotional factors in decision processes questioned the normative expectations of classical economics.

- **Interdisciplinary Collaboration:**

The collaboration between Kahneman, a psychologist, and Tversky, an economist, exemplifies the value of interdisciplinary collaboration.

Their partnership demonstrated that insights from psychology could significantly enrich economic research and theory.

- **Impact on Policy and Practical Applications:**

Kahneman's work has had practical implications, influencing policy-making and decision-making in various domains.

Concepts like prospect theory and behavioral insights have been employed in designing policies related to finance, healthcare, and environmental conservation.

- **Popularization of Behavioral Science:**

"Thinking, Fast and Slow," Kahneman's popular book, brought behavioral science to a wider audience.

The book's accessibility contributed to the popularization of key concepts, making behavioral economics more understandable and relevant to the general public.

- **Influence Beyond Academia:**

Kahneman's influence extends beyond academic circles, reaching professionals in finance, business, and public policy.

His ideas have been integrated into decision-making processes, risk management strategies, and organizational practices.

- **Continued Research and Thought Leadership:**

Even after receiving the Nobel Prize, Kahneman continued to be a thought leader in behavioral economics.

His ongoing research, writings, and public engagements contribute to shaping discussions on decision science and behavioral insights.

In summary, Daniel Kahneman's recognition and significance lie in his pioneering contributions to behavioral economics, challenging conventional economic models, and reshaping the understanding of human decision-making. His work has not only influenced academic disciplines but has also left a lasting impact on practical applications and policy domains.

Influence on Kahneman's career and field

Daniel Kahneman's career and influence on the fields of psychology and economics have been marked by several key factors:

- **Collaboration with Amos Tversky:**

The partnership with Amos Tversky was a defining factor in Kahneman's career. Their collaboration produced groundbreaking research that challenged traditional economic models.

The synergy between a psychologist (Kahneman) and an economist (Tversky) demonstrated the power of interdisciplinary collaboration in generating transformative ideas.

- **Development of Prospect Theory:**

The formulation of Prospect Theory, a seminal work by Kahneman and Tversky, revolutionized decision science by integrating psychological insights into economic analysis.

This work laid the foundation for the field of behavioral economics and had a profound impact on how scholars and practitioners understand decision-making.

- **Nobel Prize in Economic Sciences:**

The Nobel Prize in Economic Sciences in 2002 was a pinnacle moment in Kahneman's career. It not only recognized his individual contributions but also validated the significance of behavioral economics.

The prize elevated Kahneman's profile globally, contributing to increased attention and interest in the field.

- **Thinking, Fast and Slow:**

Kahneman's book, "Thinking, Fast and Slow," served as a vehicle for bringing complex psychological concepts to a wider audience.

The book's popularity contributed to the dissemination of behavioral science beyond academic circles, influencing professionals, policymakers, and the general public.

- **Shift in Economic Paradigms:**

Kahneman's work precipitated a shift in economic paradigms, moving away from strict rational choice models toward more realistic and nuanced models that account for cognitive biases and heuristics.

Behavioral economics, as influenced by Kahneman, has become an integral part of economic research and policymaking.

- **Legacy in Decision Science:**

Kahneman's legacy is evident in the lasting impact of his ideas on decision science. Concepts such as loss aversion, anchoring, and the two-system model of thinking continue to shape research and discussions in psychology and economics.

His work laid the groundwork for subsequent generations of researchers who have expanded on and applied behavioral insights.

- **Teaching and Mentoring:**

As an educator and mentor, Kahneman has influenced numerous students and researchers who have gone on to contribute to the fields of psychology and economics.

His teaching and mentorship have played a role in shaping the next generation of scholars interested in understanding the complexities of human decision-making.

- **Continued Research and Thought Leadership:**

Even after receiving the Nobel Prize, Kahneman continued to be active in research and thought leadership.

His ongoing contributions have ensured that his impact on the field remains dynamic and relevant, as he continues to explore new aspects of decision science.

In summary, Daniel Kahneman's career has been characterized by transformative collaborations, groundbreaking theories, global recognition, and a commitment to advancing our understanding of decision-making. His influence extends beyond academic boundaries, shaping both research agendas and practical applications in psychology and economics.

Chapter Five: Thinking, Fast and Slow

Thinking, Fast and Slow" is a seminal book by Daniel Kahneman, published in 2011. The book explores the two systems of thinking that govern human decision-making and offers profound insights into the cognitive processes that shape our judgments and choices. Here are key points about the book:

- **Two Systems of Thinking:**

Kahneman introduces the concept of two thinking systems: System 1 and System 2.

System 1 is fast, intuitive, and automatic, while System 2 is slow, deliberate, and analytical.

- **Heuristics and Biases:**

The book delves into the cognitive biases and heuristics that influence decision-making.

Kahneman explores how these mental shortcuts, while often efficient, can lead to systematic errors in judgment.

- **Prospect Theory:**

Kahneman elaborates on Prospect Theory, developed with Amos Tversky, which describes how people evaluate potential gains and losses.

The theory introduces the concept of loss aversion, where losses loom larger than equivalent gains.

- **Availability Heuristic:**

The availability heuristic is discussed, highlighting how people tend to rely on readily available information when making judgments.

Kahneman illustrates how this bias can lead to distorted perceptions of risk.

- **Anchoring Effect:**

The anchoring effect, where initial information (anchors) influences subsequent judgments, is explored.

Kahneman discusses how individuals can be swayed by irrelevant information when making decisions.

- **Endowment Effect:**

The book examines the endowment effect, where people tend to assign higher value to items simply because they own them.

This concept challenges classical economic assumptions about rational decision-making.

- **Regression to the Mean:**

Kahneman discusses the tendency for extreme events to regress toward the average over time.

This phenomenon has implications for understanding the natural variability of outcomes.

- **Overconfidence and Planning Fallacy:**

The book explores the psychological biases of overconfidence and the planning fallacy.

Kahneman discusses how individuals often overestimate their abilities and underestimate the time required for future tasks.

- **Application to Everyday Life:**

"Thinking, Fast and Slow" provides numerous examples and real-world applications of the concepts discussed.

Kahneman offers insights into decision-making in various contexts, from financial choices to medical decisions.

- **Impact and Popularization:**

The book has been widely acclaimed for its clarity and accessibility, making complex psychological concepts understandable to a general audience.

It has played a significant role in popularizing behavioral economics and influencing diverse fields, including business, public policy, and education.

- **Legacy:**

"Thinking, Fast and Slow" has left a lasting legacy, contributing to the public's awareness of the intricacies of human thought and decision-making.

It continues to be a foundational text in behavioral economics and cognitive psychology.

In summary, "Thinking, Fast and Slow" is a landmark work that synthesizes decades of research by Daniel Kahneman, providing readers with profound insights into the dual systems of thinking that shape our choices and the cognitive biases that influence decision-making in everyday life.

Overview of the book

Thinking, Fast and Slow" by Daniel Kahneman is a comprehensive exploration of the cognitive processes that underlie decision-making. The book provides an in-depth analysis of the two systems of thinking that govern human behavior, offering insights into the strengths, weaknesses, and biases inherent in each system. Here's an overview of the key themes and concepts covered in the book:

- **Two Systems of Thinking:**

System 1: Fast, intuitive, and automatic. It operates effortlessly and quickly, relying on heuristics and intuition.

System 2: Slow, deliberate, and analytical. It engages in rational thinking, processing information more systematically.

- **Cognitive Biases and Heuristics:**

Kahneman explores a multitude of cognitive biases and heuristics that impact decision-making, such as availability heuristic, anchoring, and overconfidence.

The book illustrates how these mental shortcuts can lead to systematic errors in judgment.

- **Prospect Theory:**

Co-developed by Kahneman and Amos Tversky, Prospect Theory challenges traditional economic models by introducing the idea that people evaluate potential outcomes based on perceived gains and losses, rather than objective values.

- **Loss Aversion:**

The concept of loss aversion, a key element of Prospect Theory, emphasizes that people tend to fear losses more than they value equivalent gains. This has profound implications for risk-taking and decision-making.

- **Endowment Effect:**

Kahneman discusses the endowment effect, where individuals assign higher value to items simply because they own them. This challenges classical economic notions of rational decision-making.

- **Overconfidence and Planning Fallacy:**

The book explores how individuals often overestimate their own abilities and underestimate the time required for future tasks, leading to overconfidence and the planning fallacy.

- **Regression to the Mean:**

Kahneman explains the phenomenon of regression to the mean, where extreme events tend to move toward the average over time. This has implications for understanding the natural variability of outcomes.

- **Availability Heuristic:**

The availability heuristic is discussed, highlighting how people rely on readily available information when making judgments, even if it is not representative of the actual probability.

- **Real-World Applications:**

Kahneman provides numerous examples and real-world applications of the concepts discussed, making the book accessible to a broad audience.

The application of behavioral economics to various fields, including finance, medicine, and public policy, is explored.

- **Thinking Slowly for Better Decisions:**

The book advocates for the importance of thinking slowly (System 2) in certain situations to overcome biases and make more rational decisions.

Kahneman provides guidance on when to trust intuition and when to engage in deliberate, conscious thought.

- **Impact on Behavioral Economics:**

"Thinking, Fast and Slow" has had a profound impact on the field of behavioral economics, popularizing key concepts and contributing to a broader understanding of decision-making.

It has influenced not only academia but also fields such as business, policy-making, and education.

In summary, "Thinking, Fast and Slow" is a seminal work that bridges the gap between academic research and a general audience, offering a rich exploration of the psychological mechanisms that shape human decision-making. The book has had a lasting impact on our understanding of cognition, biases, and the complexities of rationality.

Key concepts and insights

Thinking, Fast and Slow" by Daniel Kahneman introduces a plethora of key concepts and insights into the psychology of decision-making. Here are some of the central ideas explored in the book:

- **Two Systems of Thinking:**

System 1: Fast, intuitive, and automatic thinking that relies on heuristics and intuition.

System 2: Slow, deliberate, and analytical thinking that engages in conscious reasoning and problem-solving.

- **Prospect Theory:**

Individuals evaluate potential outcomes based on perceived gains and losses relative to a reference point.

Loss aversion: People fear losses more than they value equivalent gains.

- ## **Cognitive Biases and Heuristics:**

Availability Heuristic: Relying on readily available information, even if it's not representative of the actual probability.

Anchoring: Being influenced by initial information when making judgments.

Overconfidence: The tendency to overestimate one's own abilities and knowledge.

- ## **Endowment Effect:**

People assign higher value to items simply because they own them, challenging traditional economic notions.

- ## **Regression to the Mean:**

Extreme events tend to move toward the average over time, a phenomenon known as regression to the mean.

- **Planning Fallacy:**

Underestimating the time, costs, and risks of future actions, leading to overly optimistic planning.

- **Loss Aversion and Risk Aversion:**

Loss aversion affects decision-making, and individuals tend to be risk-averse in the domain of gains but risk-seeking in the domain of losses.

- **Integrating Systems 1 and 2:**

Optimal decision-making involves a dynamic interplay between the fast, intuitive processes of System 1 and the slow, deliberate processes of System 2.

- **Thinking Slow:**

Encourages conscious, deliberate thinking (System 2) in situations where biases and errors are likely to occur.

Recognizes the value of slowing down to make better decisions.

• **Hindsight Bias:**

The tendency to believe, after an event has occurred, that one would have predicted or expected the outcome.

• **Narrative Fallacy:**

Creating coherent and compelling stories after the fact to explain events, even if the explanations are not supported by evidence.

• **Dual-Process Theory:**

The combination of fast, intuitive thinking (System 1) and slow, deliberate thinking (System 2) provides a comprehensive model for understanding decision processes.

• **Utility and Happiness:**

Kahneman discusses the differences between experienced utility and remembered utility, shedding light on how individuals perceive and recall happiness.

- **Teaching and Training System 1:**

The potential for training System 1 to improve decision-making in certain contexts is explored, challenging the notion that System 1 is entirely fixed.

- **Experiencing Self vs. Remembering Self:**

The distinction between the experiencing self (in the moment) and the remembering self (reflecting on past experiences) and how it influences our overall sense of well-being.

"Thinking, Fast and Slow" synthesizes decades of research in psychology and behavioral economics, offering readers a profound understanding of the cognitive processes that shape human decision-making. The concepts presented in the book continue to have a lasting impact

Daniel Kahneman

on fields ranging from economics to psychology and beyond.

Chapter Six: Collaborations with Amos Tversky

The collaboration between Daniel Kahneman and Amos Tversky was a pivotal force that reshaped the fields of psychology and economics. Their partnership, spanning several decades, produced groundbreaking research that challenged conventional economic theories and laid the foundation for the field of behavioral economics. Here are key aspects of their collaborations:

- **Formation of a Dynamic Duo:**

Kahneman and Tversky began collaborating in the late 1960s when they were both faculty members at the Hebrew University of Jerusalem.

Their collaboration was characterized by a shared curiosity about the systematic errors and biases in human judgment and decision-making.

- **Synergy of Expertise:**

Kahneman, a psychologist, brought expertise in understanding human behavior and cognitive processes.

Tversky, an economist and mathematical psychologist, contributed insights from the perspective of decision theory and formal modeling.

- **Seminal Papers on Heuristics and Biases:**

Their early collaborations resulted in influential papers such as "Judgment under Uncertainty: Heuristics and Biases" (1974), which laid the groundwork for the study of cognitive biases and heuristics.

They identified and explored concepts like anchoring, availability heuristic, and representativeness heuristic.

- **Prospect Theory (1979):**

The duo's most significant contribution was the development of Prospect Theory, presented in the landmark paper "Prospect Theory: An Analysis of Decision under Risk" (1979).

This theory fundamentally challenged traditional economic models by introducing the idea that individuals evaluate outcomes based on perceived gains and losses relative to a reference point.

- **Collaborative Research Style:**

Kahneman and Tversky's research was characterized by a close collaboration that involved intense discussions, joint problem-solving, and a shared enthusiasm for exploring new ideas.

They complemented each other's skills, with Kahneman's focus on human cognition and Tversky's expertise in decision theory.

- **Interdisciplinary Impact:**

Their work bridged the gap between psychology and economics, fostering an interdisciplinary approach to understanding decision-making.

Their collaborations had a profound impact on both fields, leading to the integration of psychological insights into economic models.

- **Recognition and Awards:**

Kahneman and Tversky's collaborations gained widespread recognition within the academic community.

Although Tversky passed away in 1996, their joint contributions earned Kahneman the Nobel Prize in Economic Sciences in 2002.

- **Legacy in Behavioral Economics:**

The collaborations between Kahneman and Tversky laid the foundation for the field of behavioral economics.

Their research challenged the rational choice model and provided a more realistic understanding of how individuals make decisions.

- **Influence on Future Research:**

The work of Kahneman and Tversky continues to influence subsequent generations of researchers and has spurred a wealth of research in behavioral economics and decision science.

Concepts and experiments developed during their collaboration remain central to the study of human decision-making.

In summary, the collaboration between Kahneman and Tversky was marked by intellectual synergy, innovative research, and a transformative impact on the fields of psychology and economics. Their collective contributions reshaped the landscape of decision science and continue to inspire researchers across disciplines.

Partnership and contributions

The partnership between Daniel Kahneman and Amos Tversky was a dynamic and influential collaboration that significantly shaped the fields of psychology and economics. Their contributions, characterized by innovative thinking and groundbreaking research, continue to have a lasting impact. Here's an overview of their partnership and key contributions:

- **Formation of a Dynamic Duo:**

Kahneman and Tversky's collaboration began in the late 1960s when they were both faculty members at the Hebrew University of Jerusalem.

Their collaboration emerged from a shared interest in understanding the systematic biases and heuristics that influence human decision-making.

- ## **Seminal Papers on Heuristics and Biases:**

One of their early collaborations resulted in the influential paper "Judgment under Uncertainty: Heuristics and Biases" (1974).

This paper laid the foundation for the study of cognitive biases and heuristics, identifying key concepts like anchoring, availability heuristic, and representativeness heuristic.

- ## **Prospect Theory (1979):**

The duo's most groundbreaking contribution was the development of Prospect Theory, presented in the seminal paper "Prospect Theory: An Analysis of Decision under Risk" (1979).

Prospect Theory challenged traditional economic models by introducing the concept that individuals evaluate outcomes based on perceived gains and losses relative to a reference point.

- **Exploration of Loss Aversion:**

Their research highlighted the concept of loss aversion, where individuals tend to fear losses more than they value equivalent gains.

Loss aversion became a central theme in behavioral economics, influencing discussions on risk-taking behavior and decision-making.

- **Interdisciplinary Approach:**

Kahneman, a psychologist, and Tversky, an economist, brought complementary expertise to their collaborations.

Their interdisciplinary approach bridged the gap between psychology and economics, fostering a richer understanding of decision-making.

- **Recognition and Awards:**

Kahneman and Tversky's collaborative work gained widespread recognition within the academic community.

While Tversky, unfortunately, passed away in 1996, their joint contributions earned Kahneman the Nobel Prize in Economic Sciences in 2002.

- **Impact on Behavioral Economics:**

The Kahneman-Tversky collaboration laid the foundation for the field of behavioral economics, challenging the assumptions of classical economic models.

Their insights influenced subsequent research in behavioral economics, leading to the integration of psychological factors into economic analyses.

- **Popularization of Behavioral Science:**

The concepts developed by Kahneman and Tversky reached a broader audience through Kahneman's book "Thinking, Fast and Slow," which synthesized their key ideas for a general readership.

- **Legacy and Continued Influence:**

The Kahneman-Tversky partnership left a lasting legacy in the study of human decision-making.

Their work continues to influence researchers, policymakers, and practitioners across diverse fields, shaping discussions on rationality, biases, and heuristics.

In summary, the collaboration between Daniel Kahneman and Amos Tversky was characterized by intellectual synergy and pioneering contributions. Their work revolutionized the understanding of decision science, inspiring subsequent generations of researchers and shaping the interdisciplinary field of behavioral economics.

Tversky's influence on Kahneman's work

Amos Tversky had a profound influence on Daniel Kahneman's work, and their collaborative partnership significantly shaped the trajectory of behavioral economics. Here are key aspects of Tversky's influence on Kahneman's work:

- **Intellectual Synergy:**

Tversky and Kahneman's collaboration was marked by intellectual synergy, with each bringing unique perspectives to the partnership.

Tversky's background in mathematical psychology and decision theory complemented Kahneman's expertise in cognitive psychology.

- **Development of Prospect Theory:**

Tversky played a crucial role in the development of Prospect Theory, a groundbreaking framework for understanding decision-making under uncertainty.

Their joint work challenged traditional economic models and introduced concepts like loss aversion, which became foundational in behavioral economics.

- **Identification of Heuristics and Biases:**

Together, Tversky and Kahneman identified and explored various cognitive biases and heuristics that influence human decision-making.

Their seminal paper "Judgment under Uncertainty: Heuristics and Biases" (1974) laid the groundwork for understanding systematic errors in judgment.

- **Collaborative Problem-Solving:**

Tversky's analytical approach and Kahneman's psychological insights created a powerful combination for collaborative problem-solving.

Their discussions and joint research contributed to the formulation of innovative ideas that reshaped the fields of psychology and economics.

- **Challenging Norms in Decision Science:**

Tversky and Kahneman's collaborative efforts challenged the prevailing norms in decision science, particularly the assumptions of rational choice theory.

Their work highlighted the importance of understanding how people actually make decisions, incorporating elements of bounded rationality and cognitive biases.

- **Empirical Rigor and Formal Modeling:**

Tversky's background in mathematical psychology brought an emphasis on formal modeling and empirical rigor to their collaborative research.

Their work was not only theoretically groundbreaking but also supported by robust empirical evidence.

- **Recognition and Awards:**

While Tversky did not share the Nobel Prize with Kahneman, his influence and contributions were acknowledged by Kahneman and the wider academic community.

Kahneman often emphasized the collaborative nature of their work and the shared credit for their groundbreaking ideas.

- **Impact on Behavioral Economics:**

Tversky's influence extended beyond their collaboration, leaving a lasting impact on the trajectory of behavioral economics.

The insights generated by Tversky and Kahneman laid the foundation for subsequent research in behavioral economics, influencing scholars, policymakers, and practitioners.

- **Personal and Professional Connection:**

Tversky and Kahneman's collaboration went beyond professional connections; they developed a deep personal friendship over the years.

Their close relationship fostered an environment of trust and open dialogue, contributing to the success of their collaborative efforts.

In summary, Amos Tversky's influence on Daniel Kahneman's work was profound and transformative. Their collaborative partnership resulted in groundbreaking ideas that challenged conventional wisdom in decision science, paving the way for the establishment of behavioral economics as a major field of study.

Chapter Seven: Later Career

In the later stages of his career, Daniel Kahneman continued to be an influential figure in the fields of psychology, behavioral economics, and decision science. Here are key aspects of Kahneman's later career:

- **Post-Nobel Activities:**

Following his Nobel Prize in Economic Sciences in 2002, Kahneman remained active in research, teaching, and public engagement.

He continued to contribute to the development of behavioral economics and decision science.

- **Teaching and Academic Roles:**

Kahneman held various teaching and academic positions, sharing his knowledge and insights with students.

His impact as an educator extended beyond traditional academic settings, reaching a broader audience through lectures and public talks.

- **Authorship of "Thinking, Fast and Slow" (2011):**

In 2011, Kahneman authored the bestselling book "Thinking, Fast and Slow," which synthesized his decades of research and made behavioral science accessible to a general audience.

The book became a landmark in popular science literature and contributed to the widespread dissemination of behavioral economics concepts.

- **Public Engagement:**

Kahneman engaged in public dialogue on decision-making, biases, and behavioral insights.

His efforts helped bridge the gap between academic research and public understanding, raising awareness of the intricacies of human cognition.

- **Consultation and Advisory Roles:**

Kahneman served in advisory roles for various organizations, offering his expertise on decision science and behavioral economics.

His insights were sought after in diverse fields, including finance, public policy, and healthcare.

- **Influence on Policy:**

Kahneman's work continued to have an impact on policymaking, with policymakers recognizing the importance of understanding human behavior in shaping effective policies.

Concepts from behavioral economics, such as nudges and choice architecture, gained traction in the design of public interventions.

• **Continued Research Contributions:**

Kahneman remained actively involved in research, exploring new dimensions of decision science.

His work continued to inspire and influence subsequent generations of researchers, contributing to ongoing advancements in the understanding of human decision-making.

• **Honors and Recognition:**

Kahneman received numerous honors and awards beyond the Nobel Prize, recognizing his enduring contributions to the fields of psychology and economics.

His impact was acknowledged by institutions, societies, and fellow scholars.

- **Thought Leadership:**

Kahneman maintained a prominent role as a thought leader in the interdisciplinary intersection of psychology and economics.

His ideas and frameworks continued to shape discussions on rationality, biases, and the complexities of decision-making.

In summary, Daniel Kahneman's later career was characterized by a commitment to education, public engagement, and ongoing contributions to research. His ability to communicate complex concepts to a wide audience and his dedication to advancing the understanding of human decision-making cemented his legacy as one of the most influential figures in behavioral economics and psychology.

Continued research and publications

Daniel Kahneman's continued research and publications have extended his influential contributions to the understanding of human decision-making and behavioral economics. While I don't have real-time information on his latest activities, here are some aspects of his post-Nobel Prize research and notable publications:

- **"Thinking, Fast and Slow" (2011):**

Kahneman's book "Thinking, Fast and Slow" stands out as a comprehensive synthesis of his research, making behavioral science accessible to a broad audience.

The book became a bestseller and played a crucial role in popularizing concepts from behavioral economics.

- ## **Research on Happiness and Well-Being:**

Kahneman has explored the nuances of happiness and well-being, delving into the differences between the experiencing self and the remembering self.

His work has contributed to understanding how individuals perceive and recall their own happiness.

- ## **Contributions to Dual-Process Theory:**

Kahneman's work on the two-system model of thinking, where System 1 operates automatically and System 2 engages in deliberate thought, has been further explored and refined.

This framework remains influential in the study of decision processes.

- **Collaboration with Other Researchers:**

While much of Kahneman's early and groundbreaking work was in collaboration with Amos Tversky, he continued to collaborate with other researchers in the field.

Collaborations have expanded the scope of research and introduced fresh perspectives.

- **Research on Judgment and Decision-Making:**

Kahneman's ongoing research has explored various aspects of judgment and decision-making, including the impact of biases, heuristics, and situational factors.

His work remains central to the study of behavioral economics.

- **Application of Behavioral Insights:**

Kahneman's insights have found applications in diverse domains, including finance, public policy, healthcare, and organizational behavior.

Research in these applied areas has demonstrated the practical implications of behavioral economics.

- **Lectures, Talks, and Public Engagement:**

Kahneman has continued to engage with audiences through lectures, talks, and public appearances.

His efforts to communicate research findings to broader audiences have contributed to the dissemination of behavioral science concepts.

- **Impact on the Field:**

Beyond his own research, Kahneman's intellectual legacy is evident in the ongoing vibrancy of the fields he has influenced.

Researchers continue to build on and extend his ideas, ensuring a dynamic and evolving landscape in decision science and behavioral economics.

While I can provide information up to my last training cut-off in January 2022, for the latest updates on Daniel Kahneman's research and publications, I recommend checking academic databases, his official website, or recent publications in reputable journals.

Influence on policy and decision-making

Daniel Kahneman's influence on policy and decision-making has been significant, particularly through the application of insights from behavioral economics. Here are key aspects of his impact on policy:

- **Nudging and Choice Architecture:**

Kahneman's work, along with that of others in behavioral economics, has influenced the development of "nudging" strategies.

Nudges involve designing choices to guide individuals toward making better decisions without restricting their freedom.

- **Behavioral Insights in Public Policy:**

Concepts from Kahneman's research, such as Prospect Theory and loss aversion, have been applied in designing public policies.

Policymakers use behavioral insights to improve outcomes in areas like healthcare, finance, and environmental conservation.

- **Improving Decision Processes:**

Understanding biases and heuristics from Kahneman's research has led to interventions aimed at improving decision processes.

Efforts focus on helping individuals overcome cognitive biases and make more informed choices in areas like retirement savings and healthcare decisions.

- **Financial Regulation and Consumer Protection:**

Insights from behavioral economics have influenced financial regulations and consumer protection policies.

Understanding how individuals may behave irrationally in financial matters has led to the design of regulations that mitigate risks and protect consumers.

- **Healthcare Decision-Making:**

In healthcare, Kahneman's work has informed strategies to enhance patient decision-making.

Applications include improving communication of risks and benefits, encouraging preventive behaviors, and promoting adherence to medical treatments.

- **Default Options and Organ Donation:**

Changing default options has been a powerful application of behavioral insights.

For example, countries that automatically enroll citizens as organ donors unless they opt out have seen increases in organ donation rates.

- **Environmental Conservation and Energy Usage:**

Behavioral economics has influenced policies related to environmental conservation and energy efficiency.

Strategies include providing feedback on energy usage, leveraging social norms, and using incentives to encourage eco-friendly behaviors.

- **Criminal Justice and Legal Decision-Making:**

Behavioral insights have been applied in criminal justice settings to improve legal decision-making.

Understanding biases has led to reforms in areas such as sentencing and jury instructions.

- **Government Behavioral Insights Teams:**

Several governments have established behavioral insights teams, often known as "nudge units," to incorporate behavioral science into policy design.

These teams experiment with and implement behavioral interventions to improve outcomes in various policy areas.

- **Public Awareness and Education:**

Kahneman's efforts to communicate behavioral science to the public have increased awareness among policymakers and the general public.

Understanding the psychology of decision-making has become a crucial component in shaping effective policies.

In summary, Daniel Kahneman's influence on policy and decision-making lies in the

Daniel Kahneman

translation of behavioral economics concepts into practical applications. Policymakers around the world have embraced these insights to design interventions that consider the reality of human behavior, contributing to more effective and humane policy outcomes.

Chapter Eight: Legacy

Daniel Kahneman's legacy is profound and multifaceted, spanning the fields of psychology, economics, and public understanding of decision-making. Here are key elements of Kahneman's enduring legacy:

- **Founding Figure in Behavioral Economics:**

Kahneman is a founding figure in behavioral economics, challenging traditional economic models by integrating insights from psychology into the study of decision-making.

His work laid the groundwork for understanding how cognitive biases and heuristics shape human choices.

- **Nobel Prize in Economic Sciences (2002):**

The Nobel Prize in Economic Sciences awarded to Kahneman in 2002 not only recognized his individual contributions but also validated the significance of behavioral economics.

The prize elevated behavioral economics as a legitimate and influential field within the broader economic discourse.

- **Collaboration with Amos Tversky:**

The collaboration between Kahneman and Amos Tversky produced seminal research that continues to influence decision science.

Their partnership shaped the landscape of behavioral economics and demonstrated the power of interdisciplinary collaboration.

- **Prospect Theory and Paradigm Shift:**

Prospect Theory, co-developed by Kahneman and Tversky, represented a paradigm shift in understanding how individuals evaluate risks and make decisions.

The theory remains a cornerstone in the study of behavioral economics and decision science.

- **"Thinking, Fast and Slow" (2011):**

Kahneman's book "Thinking, Fast and Slow" became a bestseller and served as a bridge between academic research and public understanding.

The book's accessibility contributed to the popularization of behavioral economics concepts.

- **Impact on Public Policy:**

Kahneman's insights have influenced public policy, leading to the adoption of behavioral interventions in areas such as healthcare, finance, and environmental conservation.

His work has contributed to more effective and human-centered policy design.

- **Educator and Mentor:**

As an educator and mentor, Kahneman has influenced countless students and researchers.

His teachings and mentorship have played a role in shaping the next generation of scholars interested in the intersection of psychology and economics.

- **Continued Research and Thought Leadership:**

Kahneman's post-Nobel career has been marked by continued research, thought leadership, and contributions to decision science.

He has remained an active and influential figure, exploring new dimensions of human cognition.

- **Public Engagement and Communication:**

Kahneman's efforts to communicate complex psychological concepts to the public have contributed to increased awareness of behavioral science.

His public engagement has helped demystify academic research and make it accessible to a wider audience.

- **Integration of Psychology into Economics:**

Kahneman's legacy is evident in the ongoing integration of psychological insights into economic models.

The study of behavioral economics continues to evolve, with Kahneman's work serving as a cornerstone for subsequent research.

- **Recognition Beyond Academia:**

Beyond academic circles, Kahneman has gained recognition in the wider world, contributing to discussions on decision-making in various domains, including business, government, and everyday life.

In summary, Daniel Kahneman's legacy is characterized by transformative contributions to our understanding of decision-making, a paradigm shift in economic thinking, and a lasting impact on public policy and education. His work continues to shape research agendas and influence diverse fields, leaving an indelible mark on the intersection of psychology and economics.

Impact on psychology and economics

Daniel Kahneman's impact on psychology and economics is profound, shaping these fields in significant ways. Here are key aspects of his influence:

Impact on Psychology:

1. Cognitive Biases and Heuristics:

Kahneman's research, especially in collaboration with Amos Tversky, identified and explored numerous cognitive biases and heuristics that influence human decision-making.

Concepts like anchoring, availability heuristic, and representativeness heuristic became foundational in understanding the limitations of human judgment.

2. Prospect Theory and Decision Under Uncertainty:

Prospect Theory, developed by Kahneman and Tversky, revolutionized the understanding of decision-making under uncertainty.

It challenged traditional economic models by demonstrating that individuals evaluate potential outcomes based on perceived gains and losses relative to a reference point.

3. **Dual-Process Theory:**

Kahneman's distinction between System 1 (intuitive, automatic) and System 2 (deliberative, analytical) thinking became a cornerstone of dual-process theory in psychology.

This framework is widely used to explain cognitive processes and decision-making strategies.

4. **Applied Psychology:**

Kahneman's work has practical applications in various fields, including marketing, finance, and healthcare.

Understanding cognitive biases has implications for advertising, consumer behavior, and the design of interventions to improve decision processes.

5. **Happiness and Well-Being:**

Kahneman's research extended to the study of happiness and well-being, contributing to the understanding of how individuals perceive and remember their life experiences.

His work challenged traditional economic assumptions about utility and satisfaction.

Impact on Economics:

- **Behavioral Economics:**

Kahneman played a pivotal role in the development of behavioral economics, challenging the rational choice model of traditional economics.

Behavioral economics integrates insights from psychology into economic analyses, acknowledging that individuals often deviate from perfect rationality.

• Application of Prospect Theory:

Prospect Theory has had a profound impact on economic thinking, influencing how economists model decision-making under risk and uncertainty.

Concepts such as loss aversion and reference-dependent preferences are now integral to understanding economic behavior.

• Policy Implications:

Behavioral economics, influenced by Kahneman's work, has informed policy design in areas such as healthcare, finance, and environmental conservation.

Policymakers increasingly consider behavioral insights to shape interventions that align with how people actually make decisions.

- **Market Anomalies and Investor Behavior:**

Kahneman's research on cognitive biases shed light on market anomalies and deviations from traditional economic assumptions in financial markets.

Behavioral finance emerged as a subfield, exploring how psychological factors influence investor behavior and market outcomes.

- **Influence on Economic Methodology:**

Kahneman's work challenged the positivist and rationalist foundations of neoclassical economics.

His influence led to a broader acceptance of empirical research and a more interdisciplinary approach in economic methodology.

• **Teaching Behavioral Economics:**

The concepts developed by Kahneman and others in behavioral economics are now integral to economics curricula.

Students are exposed to the insights from psychology, enriching their understanding of economic decision-making.

In summary, Daniel Kahneman's impact on psychology and economics is transformative. His contributions have reshaped how scholars and practitioners understand human decision-making, influencing research agendas, policy applications, and educational approaches in both fields. The integration of psychological insights into economic models has created a more nuanced and realistic understanding of economic behavior.

Continuing influence on the field

Daniel Kahneman's continuing influence on the fields of psychology and economics remains palpable, with ongoing impact in several key areas:

- **Behavioral Economics as a Dominant Paradigm:**

Behavioral economics, catalyzed by Kahneman's groundbreaking work, continues to be a dominant and influential paradigm in both psychology and economics.

Researchers consistently build upon and extend the foundational concepts he introduced.

- **Further Developments in Decision Science:**

Scholars continue to expand on Kahneman's work in decision science, exploring new facets of cognitive biases, heuristics, and the interplay between System 1 and System 2 thinking.

Research in these areas contributes to a deeper understanding of human decision-making processes.

- **Integration of Behavioral Insights:**

Behavioral insights, derived from Kahneman's research, are increasingly integrated into diverse fields, including public policy, marketing, finance, and healthcare.

Practitioners leverage these insights to design interventions that align with human behavior.

- **Continued Research Contributions:**

While Kahneman is officially retired, his influence endures through the work of scholars inspired by his research.

Researchers continue to explore new avenues in behavioral economics, building on Kahneman's foundational ideas.

- **Teaching and Education:**

Kahneman's impact extends to the education of future generations of psychologists, economists, and interdisciplinary scholars.

Courses in behavioral economics often include his work, ensuring that students are exposed to the fundamental concepts he pioneered.

- **Practical Applications in Business and Management:**

Businesses and management practitioners draw on behavioral economics insights in areas such as organizational behavior, marketing strategy, and decision-making processes.

The understanding of cognitive biases is applied to improve decision processes within organizations.

• **Public Awareness and Outreach:**

Kahneman's efforts to communicate behavioral science to the public have contributed to increased public awareness.

His insights have become part of public discourse, influencing how individuals perceive and understand their own decision-making.

• **Ethics and Policy Design:**

Behavioral ethics, examining the ethical implications of psychological factors on decision-making, is an area that builds on Kahneman's work.

Policymakers continue to consider behavioral insights when designing policies, aiming for more effective and ethical outcomes.

- **Challenges to Traditional Economic Models:**

Kahneman's work has led to ongoing challenges to traditional economic models that assume perfect rationality.

Scholars critically examine and question assumptions, leading to a richer and more nuanced understanding of economic behavior.

- **Interdisciplinary Research:**

The interdisciplinary nature of Kahneman's work has encouraged collaboration across diverse fields. Scholars from psychology, economics, neuroscience, and other disciplines continue to collaborate, fostering a holistic approach to understanding decision-making.

In summary, Daniel Kahneman's continuing influence on psychology and economics is evident in the sustained relevance of his ideas, the ongoing expansion of research in behavioral economics, and the integration of behavioral insights into various domains. His legacy as a transformative figure in decision science endures, shaping the trajectory of research and practical applications in both academia and the broader world.

Chapter Nine: Personal Life

While Daniel Kahneman is widely recognized for his groundbreaking contributions to psychology and economics, he is a private individual, and detailed information about his personal life is not extensively available. However, here are some general aspects:

- **Birth and Early Years:**

Daniel Kahneman was born on March 5, 1934, in Tel Aviv, Mandatory Palestine (now Israel).

He spent his formative years in France during World War II, experiencing the German occupation.

- **Educational Background:**

Kahneman pursued his academic studies in psychology, earning a bachelor's degree from Hebrew University in Jerusalem and later completing his Ph.D. at the University of California, Berkeley.

- **Family:**

Kahneman is known to have a family, including a wife, Anne Treisman, who is also a highly respected psychologist. Anne Treisman passed away in 2018.

Further details about Kahneman's family life are generally kept private.

- **Collaboration with Amos Tversky:**

One of the defining aspects of Kahneman's professional life was his collaboration with Amos Tversky, which spanned several decades.

Beyond academic partnership, Kahneman and Tversky shared a deep personal friendship.

- **Later Career and Recognition:**

In the later stages of his career, Kahneman continued to be active in research, teaching, and public engagement.

His work received widespread recognition, culminating in the Nobel Prize in Economic Sciences in 2002.

- **Authorship of "Thinking, Fast and Slow":**

Kahneman authored the highly acclaimed book "Thinking, Fast and Slow," published in 2011. The book synthesizes his research for a general audience and has had a profound impact on public understanding of decision-making.

- **Retirement:**

Kahneman officially retired from Princeton University, where he held a position as a professor, after receiving the Nobel Prize.

Despite his retirement, he remained engaged in research and continued to contribute to the field.

• **Public Engagement:**

Kahneman engaged in public outreach, giving lectures, talks, and interviews to communicate the findings of behavioral science to a wider audience.

His efforts aimed to bridge the gap between academic research and public understanding.

Family and personal experiences

Daniel Kahneman, being a private individual, has not extensively shared details about his family and personal experiences in the public domain. Here are some general aspects:

- **Marriage to Anne Treisman:**

Israeli educational psychologist Irah Kahneman was Kahneman's first wife. The couple had two children together. While Lenore Shoham, his daughter, works in technology, her son suffers from schizophrenia.

Kahneman was married to his second wife, Anne Treisman, who was also a distinguished psychologist known for her work in attention and perception until she died in 2018 . The couple had a significant impact on their respective fields, making substantial contributions to psychological research.They were part-time residents of Berkeley, California as of 2014.

He and Barbara Tversky, the widow of his longtime partner Amos Tversky, reside in New York City as of 2022.

- **Collaboration with Amos Tversky:**

One of the most pivotal relationships in Kahneman's professional life was his collaboration with Amos Tversky.

Beyond academic collaboration, they developed a close personal friendship over the years.

- **Early Years in France:**

Kahneman spent part of his childhood in France during World War II, experiencing the challenges of the German occupation.

These early life experiences likely influenced his perspective and may have contributed to his interest in understanding human decision-making under uncertainty.

- ## **Contributions to Psychology and Economics:**

Kahneman's personal experiences, while not extensively documented publicly, have undoubtedly shaped his approach to research and his dedication to understanding the complexities of human cognition and behavior.

- ## **Impact on Public Understanding:**

In his later years, Kahneman became a prominent figure not only in academia but also in the public domain.

His book "Thinking, Fast and Slow" serves as a bridge between academic research and public understanding, sharing insights from behavioral science with a broader audience.

- ## **Retirement and Continued Engagement:**

After receiving the Nobel Prize in Economic Sciences in 2002, Kahneman officially retired from Princeton University.

Despite retirement, he remained active in research and continued to contribute to the field, as well as engaging in public talks and discussions.

- **Legacy and Recognition:**

Kahneman's impact extends beyond his scholarly contributions, encompassing his legacy as a transformative figure in the intersection of psychology and economics.

He is recognized not only for his intellectual achievements but also for his role in popularizing behavioral economics concepts.

It's important to note that personal details about Kahneman's life are limited, as he has maintained a degree of privacy. The focus of public information and discussions surrounding Kahneman generally revolves around his professional achievements and contributions to the fields of psychology and economics.

Balancing work and life

While specific details about Daniel Kahneman's approach to balancing work and life are not extensively documented, successful individuals often employ strategies to manage their professional and personal responsibilities. Here are some general principles that many people, including notable figures like Kahneman, consider:

- **Time Management:**

Efficient time management is crucial for balancing work and personal life. Setting priorities and allocating dedicated time for both professional and personal activities helps maintain a sense of balance.

- **Boundaries and Prioritization:**

Establishing clear boundaries between work and personal life helps prevent burnout. Prioritize tasks based on their importance and allocate time accordingly.

- **Delegation:**

Delegating tasks when possible allows individuals to focus on high-priority activities. This applies both in professional settings and within personal responsibilities.

- **Quality over Quantity:**

Emphasizing the quality of work over the quantity of hours spent can contribute to a more balanced lifestyle. This approach often leads to increased productivity and satisfaction.

- **Effective Communication:**

Communicating expectations and boundaries with colleagues, collaborators, and family members is essential. Open communication helps manage expectations and prevents misunderstandings.

- ## **Self-Care:**

Prioritizing self-care, including physical exercise, adequate sleep, and relaxation, contributes to overall well-being. Taking care of one's physical and mental health is crucial for sustained success.

- ## **Flexibility and Adaptability:**

Remaining flexible and adaptable to changing circumstances is key. Life is dynamic, and being open to adjusting schedules and plans helps navigate unexpected challenges.

- ## **Regular Breaks:**

Taking regular breaks, both during the workday and in personal time, can enhance focus and prevent burnout. Short breaks contribute to increased productivity and creativity.

• **Setting Realistic Goals:**

Setting realistic and achievable goals, both in professional and personal realms, helps maintain a sense of accomplishment without overwhelming oneself.

• **Reflection and Evaluation:**

Regularly reflecting on work-life balance and evaluating whether adjustments are needed is essential. This self-assessment allows individuals to make informed decisions about their priorities.

• **Prioritizing Family and Personal Time:**

Acknowledging the importance of family and personal time as integral components of a fulfilling life helps individuals maintain a healthy balance.

It's important to note that work-life balance is subjective and can vary based on individual preferences and circumstances.

While these principles are general guidelines, each person may find a unique approach that works best for them. Balancing work and life is an ongoing process, and individuals may need to adapt their strategies over time.

Chapter Ten: Conclusion

In conclusion, the life and work of Daniel Kahneman represent a remarkable journey through the realms of psychology and economics. From his early years, marked by experiences in wartime France, to his collaborative efforts with Amos Tversky, Kahneman has left an indelible mark on the understanding of human decision-making.

His pioneering research, including the development of Prospect Theory and the exploration of cognitive biases, has reshaped the landscape of behavioral economics. The Nobel Prize in Economic Sciences in 2002 stands as a testament to the significance of his contributions, validating the integration of psychological insights into economic models.

Beyond academia, Kahneman's commitment to public engagement, exemplified in his bestselling book "Thinking, Fast and Slow," has played a crucial role in bridging the gap between scholarly research and public understanding. His influence extends into the practical realms of policy design, organizational behavior, and various aspects of everyday life.

As a private individual, Kahneman has maintained a balance between personal and professional spheres, contributing not only to his intellectual legacy but also to a broader conversation about the complexities of work-life balance.

In reflecting on Daniel Kahneman's legacy, it is evident that his impact continues to resonate across disciplines, shaping the way we perceive decision-making, challenging conventional economic paradigms, and inspiring future generations of researchers and thinkers.

Summary of key points

Certainly! Here's a summary of key points regarding Daniel Kahneman:

- **Early Life and Background:**

Born in 1934 in Tel Aviv, Kahneman spent part of his childhood in France during World War II.

- **Educational Journey:**

Earned his Ph.D. at the University of California, Berkeley, and later became a professor at Princeton University.

- **Collaboration with Amos Tversky:**

Collaborated with Amos Tversky, forming a transformative partnership that produced groundbreaking research.

- **Prospect Theory:**

Developed Prospect Theory, challenging traditional economic models and introducing concepts like loss aversion.

- **Nobel Prize in Economic Sciences (2002):**

Awarded the Nobel Prize, validating the significance of behavioral economics.

- **"Thinking, Fast and Slow" (2011):**

Authored a bestselling book, making behavioral science accessible to a broader audience.

- **Impact on Policy and Decision-Making:**

Influenced public policy through behavioral insights, addressing areas such as healthcare, finance, and environmental conservation.

- **Balancing Work and Life:**

Maintained a balance between professional and personal life, emphasizing self-care and effective time management.

- **Continued Influence:**

Continued to contribute to research post-Nobel, influencing fields like decision science and behavioral economics.

- **Legacy:**

Transformed the fields of psychology and economics, leaving a lasting legacy through foundational research and public engagement.

In essence, Daniel Kahneman's life and work are characterized by transformative contributions to understanding human decision-making, influencing policy, and shaping the intersection of psychology and economics.

Final thoughts on Daniel Kahneman's life and contributions

In reflecting on Daniel Kahneman's life and contributions, it becomes evident that he is a pioneering figure whose impact transcends the boundaries of psychology and economics. His journey from wartime experiences in France to receiving the Nobel Prize in Economic Sciences is a testament to the transformative power of interdisciplinary collaboration and the pursuit of understanding the complexities of human decision-making.

Kahneman's partnership with Amos Tversky led to groundbreaking insights, notably Prospect Theory, which challenged traditional economic assumptions and laid the foundation for the field of behavioral economics. This paradigm shift not only earned him the highest accolades in economics but also influenced policy, public awareness, and the very way we conceptualize rational decision-making.

His commitment to public engagement, exemplified in the widely acclaimed "Thinking, Fast and Slow," demonstrates a dedication to sharing knowledge beyond academic circles. The book has not only educated millions but has also contributed to the practical application of behavioral insights in various domains.

As a private individual, Kahneman's ability to balance his personal and professional life reflects a holistic approach to well-being, reinforcing the idea that a fulfilling life extends beyond academic achievements.

In conclusion, Daniel Kahneman's life is a narrative of intellectual curiosity, collaboration, and a relentless pursuit of understanding the intricacies of the human mind. His legacy endures through the continued impact of his ideas, shaping the landscape of psychology, economics, and the broader conversation about decision-making in our complex world.

Awards and recognition

He was chosen to become a member of the National Academy of Sciences in 2001.

Despite being a research psychologist, Kahneman was awarded the Nobel Memorial Prize in Economic Sciences in 2002 for his contributions to prospect theory.

Co-winner of the 2003 University of Louisville Grawemeyer Award for Psychology alongside Tversky was Kahneman.

He was chosen to become an American Philosophical Society member in 2005.

The American Psychological Association awarded him the Outstanding Lifetime Contributions to Psychology Award in 2007.

He received an honorary doctorate on November 6, 2009, from Erasmus

University's Economics department in Rotterdam, the Netherlands.

He was listed as one of the Bloomberg 50 most influential people in global finance in both 2011 and 2012.

The American Academy of Arts and Sciences granted him the Talcott Parsons Prize on November 9, 2011.

His book Thinking, Fast and Slow won the National Academy of Sciences Communication Award for best book published in 2011 as well as the Los Angeles Times Book Award for Current Interest in 2011.

He was admitted to the Real Academia Española (Economic and Financial Sciences) in 2012 as a corresponding academician.

President Barack Obama declared Daniel Kahneman the winner of the Presidential Medal of Freedom on August 8, 2013.

He received an honorary doctorate on June 1, 2015, from McGill University in Montreal's Faculty of Arts.

In December 2018, The National Institute of Social Sciences named Kahneman a Gold Medal Honoree.

Kahneman was honored with the American Academy of Achievement's Golden Plate Award in 2019.

www.ingramcontent.com/pod-product-compliance
Lightning Source LLC
Chambersburg PA
CBHW070936260726
48661CB00003B/1009